THE
LEAD
LADDER

THE LEAD LADDER

Painlessly Turning Strangers into Clients, One Step at a Time

Marcus Schaller

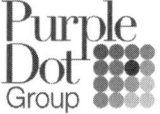

Copyright © 2005 by Marcus Schaller

All rights reserved. No part of this publication may be reproduced, distributed or transmitted in any form or by any means, including photocopying, recording, or other electronic or mechanical methods, without the prior written permission of the publisher. For permission requests, write to the publisher, addressed "Attention Permissions Coordinator" at the address below.

Purple Dot Group
20 W. 20th St., Suite 222
New York, NY 10011
Tel: (212) 822-8550
Fax: (212) 898-1385
www.purpledotgroup.com

Lead Ladder™ is a pending trademark in the United States and other countries. All trademarks contained within this work are trademarks of, or licensed to Purple Dot Group. All rights reserved. Purple Dot Group expressly forbids the use of any copyrighted material or trademark without written permission.

ORDERING INFORMATION

Quantity Sales. Special discounts are available on quantity purchases by corporations, associations and others. For details, contact Purple Dot Group at the address above.

Individual Sales. Purple Dot Group publications can be ordered direct from Purple Dot Group through our Web site at: **www.purpledotgroup.com**.

Production Management: Michael Bass Associates

Printed in the United States of America

ISBN: 0-9769881-0-0 (hardcover)
ISBN: 0-9769881-1-9 (paperback)

First Edition

Dedicated to Emily and Sam

CONTENTS

Foreword   ix

Introduction   1

CHAPTER 1
Client Goals: How Many Appointments
and Leads Will You Need?   17

CHAPTER 2
Targeting Your Market: You Can't
Be Everything to Everybody   27

CHAPTER 3
The Offer: Identifying the
Right Prospects   41

CHAPTER 4
Advertising: Where and How to
Market The Offer   63

CHAPTER 5
The Database: The Future of
Your Business   75

CHAPTER 6
Follow-up: Turning Strangers
into Clients   85

CHAPTER 7
The Success Story   91

CHAPTER 8
Applying The Lead Ladder to
Your Specific Situation   95

APPENDIX
Creating Your Marketing Plan
Step-by-Step   111

About the Author   117

FOREWORD

This book is not just about lead generation, selling products and services, or even marketing in general. It's really about people. People like you and me, each responsible for bringing in business. It's about the sales reps, consultants, real estate agents, and financial planners struggling to attract new clients. It's about the marketing executives responsible for making the cash registers ring. More than anything, it's about the people who buy your products and services.

The Lead Ladder is about earning trust. The more personable and authentic your relationship with a prospect, the easier it is to close the sale. There are no shortcuts to the process. On The Lead Ladder, trust is earned and built one rung at a time. Getting there takes generosity, commitment, and a lot of consistent action. While you will enjoy immediate rewards, the real treasures lie in the long view.

Although the characters in this story are sales professionals, The Lead Ladder is applicable for any situation in which a complex and/or expensive service or product is sold. The process is infinitely scalable, adaptable to the smallest of new businesses as well as the most established of Fortune 500 companies. It can help you whether you market and sell your own services or manage a large sales team. Only the sophistication, scale, and complexity of The Lead Ladder will be different.

For those of you committed to the success of your company or sales career, The Lead Ladder will help you get there. If you know *why* you want to succeed, this book will help you get much closer to figuring out *how*.

INTRODUCTION

The phone was silent. It had been five long weeks since the new ad was unveiled to the world. For each of those five weeks, Ted had kept vigil over his lifeless phone, not wanting to risk missing even one call.

But the calls never came. Now in week 6, Ted couldn't bring himself to accept the truth, as if admitting failure would only jinx him further. Instead, he focused on working the few sales leads he had left—always keeping one ear tilted toward the phone just in case.

A year and a half ago, Ted had been hired as a sales rep. To get a head start on his quota, he had tapped into his extensive network of friends and neighbors for leads. He was well liked and found it easy to get good referrals. His sales quickly grew as more prospects became paying clients.

As Ted became more successful, he impressed prospects and clients with fancy catered meetings and expensive "thank you" gifts. He even indulged himself by hiring a car service to take him to important meetings. Business, and life, was good.

But, after a year of tapping into his network for new clients, Ted noticed that something was wrong. Sales had slowed, and he seemed to have fewer referrals to rely on than in the past. His networking pool was getting shallow. Leads continued to flow in, but not at the rate they once had. Expenses began to catch up with revenue, leaving less money for the expensive perks he was enjoying.

Slowly, he began to phase out once seemingly necessary expenses to compensate for his lower sales. The fancy catered meetings were replaced with coffee and bagels. The executive car service was replaced with public transportation and an occasional cab ride. Still, it wasn't enough, and profits continued to shrink. Then one day, almost as quickly as they had come, Ted's profits disappeared completely.

Ted tried everything he could think of to generate more sales leads. He sweated through cold calls. He attended networking meetings and lead groups. Nothing worked. The ease with which he had once gotten leads was now gone. Instead, Ted felt like a pest. Every cold call eroded his self-esteem. People hung up on him. They treated him with suspicion and contempt. When he was able to convince someone to meet, that prospect would often cancel at the last minute, or, worse, some people never even showed up at all. His phone messages went unreturned. Every step he took felt like a struggle.

When someone would give him 10 seconds to give his pitch, he found himself stumbling over his own words. He would try to describe his company and their service, but as soon as he would get halfway through his pitch, he would hear "not interested." The harder he tried, the more people would hang up on him.

Ted knew that something would have to change if he was going to succeed. He realized that the reason he had been so successful in the past was the source of his leads. He had received referrals to people who needed what he had to offer. Since they already knew what it was that he did, it was easy to sell. And, most important, most of these appointments were friendly and comfortable, making it much easier to close new deals.

But now it was totally different. He could no longer rely on referrals for new business. He would have to go out and actively seek clients. And in doing so, he had lost the advantages he had once enjoyed. He had no idea who to focus his attention on, since nobody would tell him whether they had the problem that he solved. Because he no longer had a way to identify the best potential prospects, he wasted a lot of time and energy pursuing anyone who would listen. Also, he no longer experienced a personal connection with his prospects, which made his consultations uncomfortable at best and downright hostile at worst.

In a last-ditch effort to attract new clients, Ted decided to play the numbers game and hope for the best. He took a gamble and spent a quarter of his annual marketing budget on a full-page ad in a local magazine.

In the meantime, sales continued to plummet. Even the bagels and coffee were now gone since few clients were around to eat them anyway, and the occasional cab rides were phased out altogether.

Today, five weeks after it was published, the ad was a complete flop. Ted had spent thousands of dollars with nothing to show for it. Then things went from bad to worse. The phone rang. It was Mr. Mancini, Ted's boss.

"What happened?" asked Mr. Mancini. "How did you go from having more business than you could handle to suddenly falling off the face of the earth?" Ted's face grew paler as he listened. "And, more important, what are you going to do about it? Whatever it is, I suggest that you figure it out, and soon!"

Ted hung up the phone, his mouth dry. He sat and stared at the wall, silently pondering his options. The more he thought about what he needed to do, the more confused he got.

Ted thought about how simple the challenge appeared on the surface, yet how difficult finding the answers seemed to be. He needed help. He thumbed through his address file, trying to think of who he knew who might be able to help him out. He stopped when he came across Steve's name.

Steve had been Ted's next-door neighbor for years, and in that time they had become good friends. Steve was also in sales and had been able to almost triple his company's revenue in less than five years. If anyone would know what to do, it was Steve.

Ted called Steve and invited him to lunch. At the restaurant, Ted couldn't hide his frustration. He told Steve everything that had happened. When he was done, Steve simply smiled and suggested that they finish lunch and take a walk; some fresh air would help them think.

"Before I can help you," said Steve as they walked, "you need to understand that there is no silver bullet—no single answer to your problem. In order to figure this out, you're going to have to look at your approach in an entirely different way than you may be used to. Only then will you be able to turn this around."

Ted thought about when things were better, when sales leads seemed to flow in on a nice, comfortable, consistent basis—back to a time when prospects treated him with respect, not as an annoyance. He missed those days so badly. All he wanted was to get back to feeling good about his ability to work with people and generate business.

Ted nodded. "Whatever it takes. If you can help me through this, I'll give 100 percent and focus completely on whatever I have to do to get back on track."

Steve smiled and continued. "All right, so what's making this so hard?"

Ted thought about the challenges preventing him from attracting new clients.

"The biggest problem that I'm facing is that people treat me like a stranger, a pest. I know that if I can only reach the right prospects, and get them to really sit down with me and tell me about their needs, then I'll be able to sell like I used to. I don't know who to focus my attention on, so I wind up approaching everybody, since I have no idea who has the problem that I solve. It's exhausting."

"What was different back then?" asked Steve, although he already knew the answer. He wanted Ted to say it first.

"I guess the main difference was how prospects acted around me, not to mention my own comfort level with them. I mean, back then, I would get a referral from a friend or client. There was a reason for me to talk with them. On top of that, because they were personally referred, meetings with these prospects were easy and relaxed. We would simply talk. I would ask questions about their situation, and they would answer me openly."

"Why do you think that was?" Steve asked.

"I think it was simply because they trusted me to some extent," Ted replied, "because I had been referred to them by a friend. Since they trusted me, it was easy to get them to open up to me. Sometimes it would be obvious that I did not have the right solution for them, in which case I would usually refer them to someone who did. But for the most part, once they let me know their problem, I would be able to lay out a solution for them and close the deal. It was almost easy."

"And what's different now?"

Ted let out a sigh of exasperation. "Now it's torture. Because my referrals have slowed, I'm finding myself needing to actively market to strangers, and the feeling is completely different. If they talk with me at all, it's in a guarded way, like they're afraid of letting me in. I feel subhuman, like some bug that spends his days getting under people's skin. It's horrible."

Steve sat back. He had been through this phase himself. "So what is the most important thing that you need to do in order to get back to the kind of selling you once enjoyed?"

"Obviously, I have to change the way that people perceive me."

"Exactly. Let's get back to that later. What other challenges are you having?"

"Well," Ted began, "the other challenge I can think of is how hard it seems to communicate what it is that I do in a way that clients care about. I mean, I can talk about the company all day, but every time I get into it, it seems like prospects glaze over. I just lose them. I think about how much money I charge and our competition, and all those things seem easy enough to solve if I were able to capture the real essence of what it is we do. And I don't mean in the typical way, but in a way that translates instantly to a prospect and gets them to want to know more about me and what I can do for them."

"So, let's figure it out. What is it about what you are actually selling that matters to your prospects?"

"Well, they care about our company and its history, and...."

"Wait," Steve interrupted. "No, they don't."

"Of course they do. I mean, why would they use us unless they thought that we could solve their problem?"

"But that's just it," Steve said. "You just said it: It's The Solution to The Problem, not your company—at least not at the beginning."

> **The Problem:** *What your customers are willing to pay you to solve*
> **The Solution:** *The only reason your business exists*

"What do you mean?" asked Ted.

"Think about it. When you first hear about a service or product, do you really care about the company that sells it? When you get a brochure, do you read it from cover to cover, looking to learn everything you can about the organization and the people in it?"

"Well, no, actually." Ted thought about the question for a moment. "I guess what I am usually more interested in is what that company can do to help me, more than information about the company itself."

"And what have you been doing?" Steve asked. "What's your primary marketing message been?"

Ted saw where his friend was going. He thought back to his recent failed ad. It consisted of a logo, a tagline that read "Committed to Excellence," and a paragraph of copy about why his company was the best choice in its industry. He pictured the ad in his head and could not remember it saying anything about The Problem that his customers experienced or The Solution that Ted's company provided.

"It's been all about us!" Ted shouted.

Steve snapped his fingers. "It's had nothing at all to do with the one thing that you as a business exist for, that every business exists for: solving people's problems. You need to focus your marketing message on The Problem and The Solution you provide."

Ted thought about The Problem that his company solved and realized that Steve was right—they existed only to provide The Solution to that problem. Until that was clear, nothing else mattered, not their logo, their corporate image, their brand identity, or Ted's background and education. That was all irrelevant without a crystal-clear understanding of why their customers needed them in the first place.

Steve continued. "You need to package and promote The Solution in a clear enough way so as to attract the people who have The Problem. One that's cost-effective, simple to execute, flexible, and repeatable. Figure that out, and you'll be back on track. You've been approaching your marketing from the wrong perspective—*your* perspective. No wonder your ad flopped!"

Ted felt a wave of relief. Even though his recent failed ad cost him so much money, what really got under his skin was not knowing why it hadn't worked. Now he understood, and as he and Steve continued walking, he vowed never to make the same mistake again.

"All the challenges you mentioned exist because you've been trying to promote and market your company with a one-step approach," Steve explained. "It's too complex and involved to accomplish that. Since you've been so impatient, you were unwilling to think about it from the prospect's point of view, people who are very busy and being constantly bombarded with marketing messages. All of your advertising and promotional attempts have been about you—your brand, your expertise—instead of about your customers and their problems.

"Then, to make matters worse, you've been assuming that one ad or cold call will compel people to invite you into their busy lives to be sold to. As a result, people treat you like an intrusion. To them, you're just another stranger trying to sell them something. What chance do you really have by approaching people that way?"

"Obviously, slim to none," Ted admitted.

"Exactly! It's like getting people to make a standing jump from the ground to a five-foot ledge—it can be done, but it's difficult. What you need to do is to break down the process into steps, like rungs on a ladder. By making it easy to climb rung by rung, more people can and will make the trip."

Steve and Ted walked back to Ted's office, where Steve walked over to a flip chart, picked up a pen, and drew a simple ladder. "Think of it like a Lead Ladder. At the ground level, the bottom of your ladder is the market for your service. They've never heard of you before. You're just another company trying to get them to buy something they probably don't need. At the top are your clients. What you have to figure out is how to get as many people up The Lead Ladder as possible. And in order to do that, you need to figure out how many rungs you'll need. Then you can simply focus on getting as many people on the first rung as possible, and then as many people to the second rung, then the third, et cetera.

> *The Lead Ladder:*
> *A system of painlessly turning strangers into clients*

"Your Lead Ladder will painlessly transform lots of strangers into clients by consistently doing three things very well. Each of these is simple, but none of them is easy."

"What are they?" Ted asked.

"Well, in order to painlessly transform lots of strangers into clients, you need to first **identify** those people who are the most likely prospects for your product or service—before your competition reaches them. Then you need to **differentiate** yourself as an adviser, not just another salesperson. Finally, you will have to **personalize** your relationship with your leads by giving them reasons to let you into their lives. The higher the rung, the more personal the relationship will get. Once you do each of these three things, you will have built enough trust with the right prospects to get on with the business of solving The Problem and closing the deal."

"You're right," Ted remarked. "I mean, the great thing about the referrals I used to get was that they tended to be for people who needed what I had to give. And since they came from a friend, the prospect was much easier to talk with. They would treat me with respect. And since they would take the time to meet with me and discuss their issues, I was

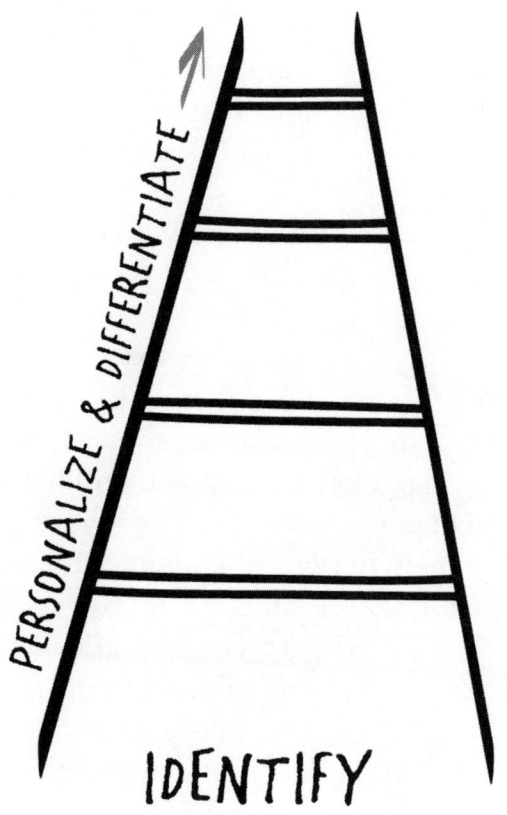

able to help more people and therefore close a lot of sales."

"That's right," Steve said. "And now you're just another salesperson. No wonder you're frustrated. What you need to do is actively create leads that have the same characteristics as your referrals.

"But before you can do that, you need to take a look at your business in a completely new way, from the perspective of your customers, not yourself. You need to answer some very important questions about what you want, where you are today, who you want to attract, how you'll attract them, and, finally, how you'll keep them moving up The Lead Ladder until they become paying clients. You need to figure out what the primary parts of your lead generation marketing plan will be. Without that, your ladder will be rickety and fragile. It will lack substance. Worst of all, it will not really go anywhere. It'll just be a random series of guesses and offers. And from the tone of your voice earlier, I think that you're pretty sick of guessing."

Ted nodded. "Boy, you got that right."

"You want something that you can create relatively quickly, get results, and then build on and improve," Steve said. "Building your Lead Ladder will bring everything together and generate the amount of sales you need to be successful."

"Sounds great!" Ted replied, feeling real optimism for the first time in weeks. He motioned for his friend to take a seat while he got comfortable behind his desk. "Where do I start?"

Chapter 1

CLIENT GOALS
How Many Appointments and Leads Will You Need?

Steve took off his jacket and relaxed in his chair. "The first thing you need to figure out is your general sales goal," he began. "One thing that I've learned over the past few years is that before I can achieve something, I need to have a pretty clear idea of what it is. Otherwise, I'm just taking random action and hoping for the best. After all, if you're going to build a Lead Ladder, you'll need to know how many people you want to get to the top and become clients. If you don't know that, how will you ever figure out how many people you need to get on the ladder to begin with?

"Those numbers will have a major influence on what kind of marketing you need to focus on," he explained. "If you only need five new clients a year, you can probably reach that goal through targeted networking, speaking, and direct mail. On the other hand, if you decide that you really need more than 50 new clients a year, then those approaches may not be enough. In that case, you'll most likely need to add more efficient forms of advertising to reach far more people. Either way, you need to figure out what it is you want first, before spending another dollar on an ad or going to one more networking event."

Ted and Steve spent the rest of that afternoon discussing Ted's sales goals. Steve drew a cone on the flip chart with four numbers next

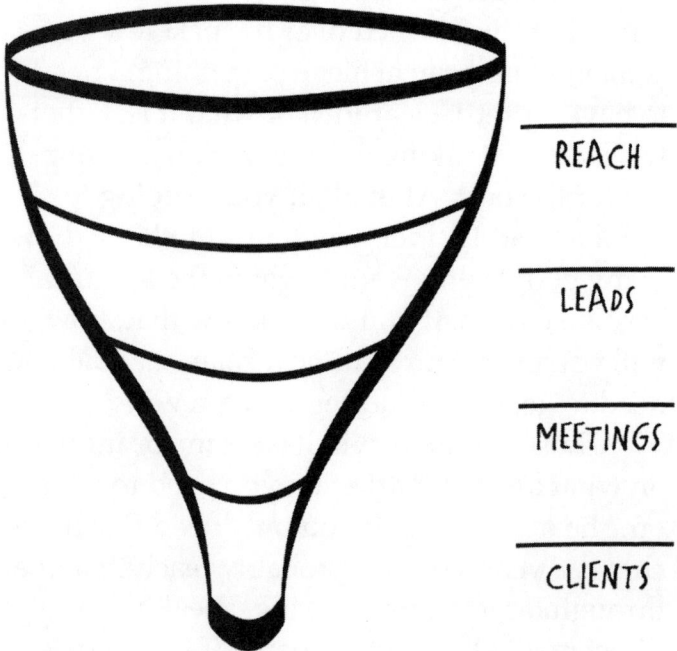

to it, each representing a target that Ted would need to hit.

"All right," Steve said as he pointed to the flip chart, "so we agree on the following things. We know that you want to gross $200,000 in commissions over the next year." They had come up with that figure based on the amount of total sales that Ted knew he could generate. Ted also knew that it was a figure that would get him back on track.

Steve continued. "And we know that your average sale is worth about $20,000 in commissions. So basically, in order to reach your revenue goal of $200,000, you need to close 10 clients at $20,000 each."

"Piece of cake," Ted said.

Steve chuckled. "I know. It seems like a big hill to climb. But you've done it before. At least you now have a target. Even if the numbers are off a little bit, like if the average commission per client is $17,000 instead of $20,000, you'll still be in the ballpark."

Ted nodded. "You're right. It seems like a lot, but it really isn't that bad."

"I know you can do it," Steve said. He then pointed at the next number on the model, directly above Ted's client goal of 10. "Now the next number. We know from your track record that you generally close about half of the prospects you meet with. That number might go higher or lower, depending on the quality of your leads and how good you are at qualifying your leads. But generally, 50 percent is the number you're comfortable with. That means that in order to land 10 clients, you need to meet with about 20 prospects."

"That's totally doable," added Ted. "I mean, that's about two a month. I'm not sure yet how we're going to generate that many appointments, but assuming we can, then an appointment every other week is something I can easily handle."

"Exactly. And if your closing rate is a little lower than we hope, you'll have the time to easily double the number of appointments you go on. That just leaves us with the challenge of figuring out how to attract those prospects to begin with. Which brings me to our next number."

Steve pointed to the number on the flip chart directly above the number of appointments Ted would need. "Now, we know that you're going to have to attract a certain number of leads to get 20 appointments. Let's just go with the assumption that you'll need roughly 10 leads for every appointment. That means that in order to get 20 appointments, you'll need to generate roughly 10 times that, or 200 leads."

"But how?" Ted interrupted. All these numbers seemed easy to talk about, but they were just empty numbers. Ted still couldn't visualize how he would attract all those hypothetical leads.

"Relax, I don't know yet," Steve replied. "Let's focus now just on figuring out the what and why. The how will come later."

Steve pointed to the top and final number on the flip chart. "Now comes the really tricky part. In order to generate 200 leads, you'll need to reach a certain number of people, depending on how you advertise. For example, if you use

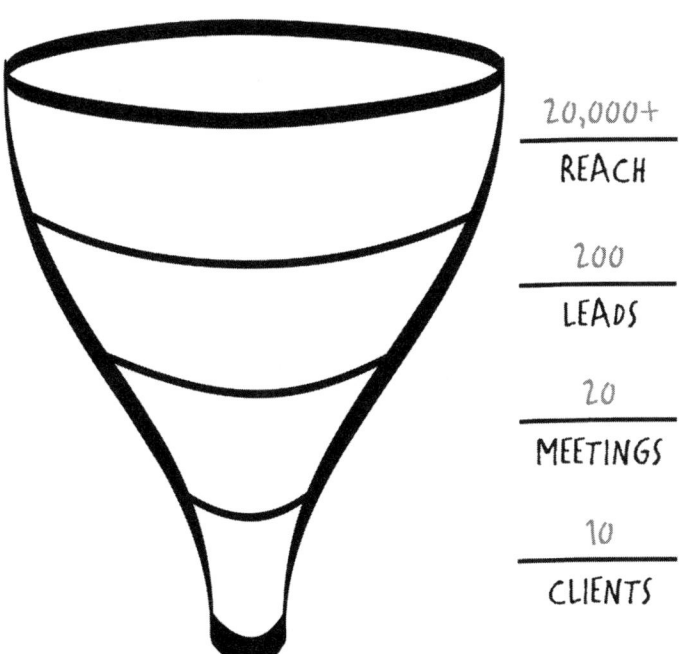

direct mail and get a 1 percent response rate, that means that you'll need to send 20,000 mailers in order to generate 200 leads. Remember, that's over the course of a year, so it would be fewer that 1,700 mailers a month."

"OK. You're right, if I can get a 1 percent return. But what if I can't? Or what if I need more clients and therefore have to reach a lot more people?"

"That's the whole reason we're doing this," Steve explained. "If you did decide you needed more clients, then direct mail may not be the most efficient way to reach larger numbers of people. In that case, you may have to consider some other form of advertising. But as it stands, it makes sense that if you stick with the goal of 10 clients from 20 appointments from 200 leads, then you'll need to reach at least 20,000 people. If you can do that with direct mail, then great. If you can find a more cost-efficient method, even better. That's something that we'll deal with later. But, there's one thing that this number sheds a lot of light on."

"What's that?" asked Ted.

"Why you've been having so little success relying on networking and cold calling. Looking at these numbers, it's no wonder why you couldn't get the level of business you had hoped for. Take networking, for example. How many events did you go to so far this year?"

Ted thought about it for a minute, adding in his head. "I'm not exactly sure, but I think it was about 20."

"And how many people did you meet at each?"

"About 20 people per event."

"OK, so that's a total of 400. And out of those 400, how many people had The Problem that your company solves?"

"I'm not sure. I just now figured out that I need to focus on The Solution as my primary message. But if I had to guess from the industries these people were in, that out of 400 people I met, only 20 or so were even in the ballpark."

"And out of those 20 people, how many did you actually get an appointment with?"

"Only two. And I know what your next question will be," Ted said with a sigh, "and the answer is that I got one client."

"One client," Steve yelled out, "after all those meetings and schmoozing and everything else! And you were upset about why nothing was working? Now it makes perfect sense. It's not that networking is bad or a waste of time. It's just that the numbers didn't add up. You couldn't possibly have reached the number of people you needed to in order to generate the leads, appointments, and clients you wanted."

Ted nodded. "So, before we had really figured out these numbers," he said, "I spent a lot of time and energy on promotional tactics that really had no chance of bringing me a significant distance to my goals. And now that we took the time to figure it out, to decide how many clients I really want, then how many appointments, and finally how many leads I need to generate, we're left with a much clearer picture of the reach I need to have with my marketing, which in turn will help narrow down my marketing tactics."

"Bingo," Steve replied. "Just having the client goal helps narrow down your choices of how and where to market your company as far as numbers and reach is concerned. The next step is to figure out exactly *who* it is that you want to reach and *why* they are the best candidates for your products and services. In other words, you need to target your market."

CHAPTER 1 REVIEW

1. What is a typical client worth in short-term sales?

2. What are your gross sales goals for the upcoming 12 months?

3. Divide the answer for question 2 by the answer for question 1. This will give the approximate number of clients you need to close to reach your projected sales goal.

4. Next, estimate the number of presentations or appointments needed to close each new client. If you don't know your closing rate offhand, simply use a number that you think is realistic.

5. Now estimate the number of leads you'll need to get this number. Again, if you don't know your own lead to appointment rate, that's OK. Just use 10 for now.

Consider that for every one lead you generate, you need to get your message in front of at least 100 people. This can be through advertising, direct mail, PR, or networking. The point is, if you need 300 leads, you'll most likely need to reach at least 30,000 people. In some cases, such as magazine advertising, you may have to reach as many as 120,000 to generate 300 leads.

The reason these numbers are so critical is simple: If you need to generate 300 leads a year, but all you do is attend networking meetings twice a month (assuming you meet even as many as 10 people at each one), you are only getting your message in front of 240 people. At that rate, it will be impossible to reach your lead generation goals, not to mention your overall sales goals.

Chapter 2

TARGETING YOUR MARKET
You Can't Be Everything to Everybody

Ted had always assumed that everyone needed his company's products and services, and therefore it made sense to cast the widest net possible. But now that he was building his marketing approach from scratch, it was time to reevaluate his strategy. He and Steve met at his office the next morning, and after a couple of strong cups of coffee, they began to tackle the question of how and even whether Ted would pick a target market.

> **Target market:** *A demographic group, industry, or set of people with similar needs or situations*

Steve began. "If you want the easiest way to get more people onto your Lead Ladder," he said, "then you have to ask yourself whether it makes sense to continue with your old approach—you know, simply putting yourself out there to whoever will listen."

"But, the problem is that I don't know whether I can afford to narrow my focus. What am I supposed to do? Pick one market and ignore the rest?" Ted asked.

"I understand your concern. But at the same time, you've been exhausting yourself trying to be everything to everybody. Not only has it been hard to actually service so many different kinds of customers, but one of the reasons your marketing message is so weak and ineffective is that you're trying to spread it too thin—not really focusing it on any particular need. It's been hurting you in ways you didn't understand until recently."

"But what if I pick the wrong target market? What then? Or what if I meet a great prospect and they're not part of our niche? Should I really be willing to sacrifice opportunities at this point?"

"That's just the thing! From what you've told me, you have already been sacrificing too many opportunities by not having a clear idea of who you're trying to reach. You've been relying on pure luck to find clients, rather than make your own luck through some kind of reasonable plan and idea of what it is you do and who you do it for."

"I don't know if I buy it," Ted said. "Why can't I serve a broader market?"

> *You have already been sacrificing too many opportunities by not having a clear idea of who you're trying to reach.*

Steve thought about Ted's question. Why couldn't he serve "the world," and wouldn't doing so increase his chances of attracting more clients? It was an attitude that used to make sense to him, but now he knew that it was a mistake. Steve was determined to help Ted understand why.

Steve stood up and drew a big circle in the center of the flip chart.

"If this circle represents all possible customers, in every industry and demographic, what would prevent you from reaching them all?"

It seemed a ridiculous question. Ted already knew that he could never reach every possible customer in the world, let alone his own town. He decided to play along anyway.

"Well, to reach all of them, I would probably have to spend a tremendous amount of money—money that I obviously don't have."

"What else?" asked Steve, writing a big dollar sign on the flip chart.

"Time and energy, too. I mean, I can only be in so many places at once."

"Keep going." Steve wrote *time* on the board.

"I can't think of another."

Steve smiled. "What about your message? We talked about how your marketing used to be about you instead of the customer, and how you need to focus your message to be about The Problem that you solve. If you think about all the different types of customers in the world, is it reasonable to assume that they all look at The Problem the same way or with the same urgency?"

"I guess not," Ted replied. He could already see where this was going.

Steve wrote "clarity of marketing message" on the board, next to the dollar sign and "time." He then pointed to the big circle that represented all of Ted's potential customers.

"Since we both agree that you can't afford to market to the whole circle," he said, "and even if you could, you don't have the time and energy to be everywhere and do everything at once, then we know that at the very least, you would have to limit your marketing to a much smaller section of the total possible market, right?"

Ted nodded.

Steve drew a very small circle randomly within the large circle. He stepped back to look at his drawing, and then continued his thought.

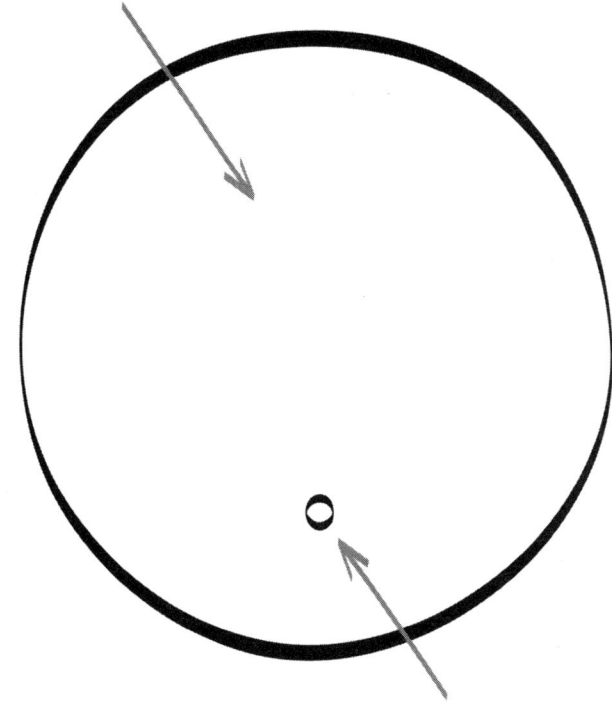

"And if you're going to market to a much smaller section of the whole, wouldn't it make sense that the customers in that particular section should have as much in common with each other as possible? Won't your marketing be that much more effective, because you can place only so many ads and send so many mailers, if it's directed toward customers who share similar views on The Problem you solve?"

Your marketing will be that much more effective if it's directed toward customers who share similar views on The Problem you solve.

"Look at it this way," Steve explained. "If you mail out 2,000 sales letters a month, does it make sense to rent lists in 10 different industries or demographics, with no regard for whether your message speaks more to one than the other? Again, based on the assumption that you only have the money, time, and energy to communicate with a limited market to begin with, doesn't it make sense that you choose one or two where you have the highest chance of success?"

"I guess so, but how would I possibly choose?" Ted was still skeptical, but his friend's point made sense. He knew that his biggest marketing problem had to do with clarity. It didn't make a lot of sense to continue to pour money into an unfocused marketing approach.

"Well, we also know that people tend to hire specialists—businesses that cater to a specific need and that understand their customers better than anyone. With that in mind, I think the first place to look is your own experience. Let's look at your past clients and ask ourselves where the similarities are, and use that as a starting point to figure out where it makes most sense to specialize by leveraging your experience."

> *People tend to hire specialists—businesses that cater to a specific need and that understand their customers better than anyone.*

With that, Ted started writing a list of all his past clients, including notes about their specific problems that he solved as well as their demographics. When he was done, the answer to Steve's question became obvious. Ted had worked with 10 types of clients, but three stood out as the most common.

"OK," said Ted. "We're down to three. Now what?"

"I think that the answer, or part of the answer, is going to come when we more clearly define The Problem you solve. Once we know that, you need to ask yourself which of those three groups has that problem and values The Solution most."

The two men brainstormed and came up with a simple, one-sentence description of The

Problem that Ted solved. Steve wrote the names of each of the three target markets on the flip chart, and they started brainstorming questions that would help them narrow down Ted's choices. Each market choice that fit the answer to the question would get a check mark underneath it.

- Do customers in this market experience The Problem for which we offer The Solution? Is The Problem big enough for them to want to pay our fee? Can they pay our fee?

- Do we have adequate experience or a competitive advantage in this market?

- Do we already have market leaders or well-known players as clients?

- Is the market underserved?

- How large is the market? Are we limited to a very small local market, or can we serve nationally or even internationally?

- What media, advertising opportunities, and mailing lists are available to reach this market? In other words, how easy or hard will it be to get our message in front of the right people?

After the last question, they looked up at the board to see the results. Out of the three possible markets that Steve wrote based on Ted's experience one stood out. It had by far the most check marks next to it. This one market had all the necessary ingredients. Ted knew that customers in that market experience major issues with The Problem and would be willing and able to pay handsomely for The Solution. He knew that he had more than enough experience serving that market and had some very recognizable names as past clients, which would give him a competitive advantage. He also realized that this particular market was underserved, since most of his competitors were trying to be everything to everybody. He knew that the market was very large and that enough people in that market lived close by. Finally, Ted rattled off a list of magazines, trade shows, and industry events that catered to this particular market. Reaching them through several methods would be easy.

"What if I'm referred to a prospect in a different market? Do I ignore an opportunity just because it doesn't fit into my strategy?" Ted asked.

Steve laughed. "Of course not! The whole point of targeting your market is to attract more leads by focusing your efforts. When prospects find you, and they will, consider it a bonus. The difference is that you won't be wasting your marketing resources—your money, time, and message—trying to be everything to everybody."

> *The whole point of targeting your market is to attract more leads by focusing your efforts.*

When all was said and done, Ted knew that he would have a much easier time targeting one lucrative market, and by serving this market well, he would more easily attract referrals to people in other markets.

"So," Ted asked, "how does this relate to The Lead Ladder?"

"Well, before we could decide how many rungs your Lead Ladder would need, or what kind of offers you need to create in order to move people from the bottom to the top of the ladder—before we could do any of that, we needed to know who you would be targeting. Company size, consumer demographics, and industry needs will determine how The Lead Ladder is constructed. Without knowing who you are trying to market to, we would have little idea of how to structure your marketing and offers in the most effective way."

> *Company size, consumer demographics, and industry needs will determine how The Lead Ladder is constructed.*

"Which then leads to my next question," Ted added. "Now that we know approximately how many leads I need to attract and what target market I'm going to focus on, how will I get people on the first rung of The Lead Ladder?"

"To generate the most leads possible," answered Steve, "just advertising your company won't cut it. You need a tangible offer, something that will **identify** the right prospects and get them on your Lead Ladder. You need to put yourself in the mind of someone in your target market, someone with The Problem that you solve, and figure out what would get their attention."

> *To generate the most leads possible, you need a tangible offer, something that will **identify** the right prospects and get them on your Lead Ladder.*

CHAPTER 2 REVIEW

Your business is probably very well suited for certain markets over others. Current client mix, experience, and market opportunities should all be taken into account to help you decide which markets to focus on and how much of your resources to spend on each one.

1. Clearly define The Problem that you solve. If there are many problems that you can solve, which is the most valuable?

2. Now express it in one sentence.

3. How do you solve The Problem?

4. How can you do it differently?

5. Who is your competition?

6. How does your competition approach its market?

7. What is keeping some of your market from using your service?

8. What markets have you served?

9. What markets would you like to serve?

10. For each market you want to serve, answer the following questions:

    - Do you have adequate experience or a competitive advantage with this market?

    - Do you have any large, well-known clients in this market?

- Is the market saturated or underserved?

- Does this market experience The Problem?

- Is the market willing and able to pay for The Solution?

- How large is the market? Are you limited to a local area, or can you serve nationally?

- What mailing lists and targeted media are available to reach this market? Is it easy to get your message in front of the right people?

Chapter 3

THE OFFER
Identifying the Right Prospects

The next day, Ted met Steve back at the office with renewed enthusiasm, even though he knew that their next challenge was very difficult. How would he get people onto the first rung of his Lead Ladder? Ted looked forward to getting some insight into what his customers would really want. Once he had a better idea of that, he would have a much easier time getting more people onto The Lead Ladder.

"I thought about this all night, and I'm still confused about how I'm going to attract leads in the first place," Ted admitted.

"The Offer," Steve answered, "is what you will use to generate leads. The primary goal of The Offer is simply to **identify** the most likely prospects. Some will sign up with you right away, but most will need to be followed

> *The Offer: The hook that identifies and attracts sales leads*

up with in order to be converted into clients. You'll need to direct them up The Lead Ladder, one rung at a time."

With that, Steve began writing on the flip chart.

"The first question we need to answer is, what is valuable to your market? Whatever The Offer will be, it must be something that prospective customers will actually want, something that they feel is worth their attention."

"Makes sense," commented Ted. "That explains why nobody requested my brochure. It was all about the company instead of the customer."

"Exactly. Whatever The Offer will be, it must be about the *customer*. Second, because the goal of The Offer is to identify the most likely prospects, the content must be relevant to The Problem that you solve.

> *Whatever The Offer will be,*
> *it must be about the **customer**.*

"I remember a trade show that I went to last month," Steve continued. "This one payroll company was raffling a free Hawaiian trip to attract people to its booth. If you think within the context of identifying prospects, the problem with a payroll company using a free vacation to generate leads is that vacations have nothing at all to do with payroll, or The Problem that a good payroll company solves for its customers. Imagine how much time the sales reps wasted with vacation seekers, instead of spending that time with much more qualified and relevant prospects. In fact, how would they even have known the difference?"

"They wouldn't have," Ted said with a smile. He'd seen this sort of approach at lots of trade shows himself.

"The Offer has to promise The Solution to The Problem that your business solves," Steve said. "That way, it has the greatest chance of being relevant to the right customers, and it will identify those people with The Problem that you solve, meaning that the list of people on the first rung of The Lead Ladder will be much easier to convert into prospects and then into clients."

> *The Offer has to promise The Solution to The Problem that your business solves.*

"So I want to make sure that I'm focusing on the right people, rather than wasting a lot of time and energy on those that don't experience The Problem that I solve."

"You got it. Also, The Offer should generate an immediate response. When you advertise or send out a mailer or exhibit at a trade show, you'll have only one shot to get the right people to request The Offer."

"You're right," added Ted. "Otherwise, I'm just wasting money on advertising and direct marketing, trying to get my 'brand' out. I need each campaign to be measurable, and the more prospects I get to request The Offer from each individual ad or mailer, the more measurable and effective my marketing will be."

Steve nodded. "Another job of The Offer is to change your service from an invisible, abstract concept into something tangible—something that can be touched, felt, and held. All of these sensory clues can give people a distinct impression of the quality of your service.

"Most important, The Offer should demonstrate your expertise in a way that helps people before they even become clients. *Showing* people how good you are is always better than telling people how good you are and will help **differentiate** you as an adviser, rather than just another salesperson."

> *The Offer should demonstrate your expertise in a way that helps people before they even become clients.*

"But what should The Offer be?" Ted asked. "There are so many ways that I can package The Solution. Should I use a consultation, or what about a seminar? How do I choose?"

"Well, when it comes to lead generation, all offers are not created equal," Steve replied.

> **Hard offer:** *An offer that requires some level of commitment from the prospect*
> **Soft offer:** *An offer that requires little or no effort or risk for the prospect*

"There are two basic categories of lead generation offers, *soft offers* and *hard offers*. A hard offer is attractive to people who are familiar with your company and are in the market for your solution right away. These are prospects who may be current users of similar services or new users looking for an immediate solution. Either way, the types of prospects who will be attracted to hard offers will generally buy sooner than later. Oftentimes, getting a response to a hard offer means that your ad or mailer simply crossed someone's path at the right place and the right time.

"Hard offers can include consultations, paid seminars, a discount on a purchase, or an invitation to visit a showroom. They involve some kind of commitment on the part of the prospect, in either time, money, or both.

*Hard offers involve some kind of
commitment on the part of the prospect,
in either time, money, or both.*

Steve took a couple of gulps from his water bottle before continuing. "The obvious advantage to using a hard offer is that these leads will be relatively easy to close. They are in the market for your service and are usually looking for one good reason to buy now. Closing these kinds of leads usually involves little more than making it easy for them to buy.

"There are, however, some disadvantages to relying on hard offers," Steve added. "In general, the harder your offer, the fewer responses you will receive because it will appeal to only a portion of possible prospects. A hard offer is like expecting someone to make a standing jump from the ground to the fourth rung of The Lead Ladder. It can be done, but most people will be unwilling to make that leap. The apparent risk of wasting time or being sold to may be just too high at that stage for them, especially if they have never heard of you or your company before.

"Soft offers, on the other hand, can generate a much higher response rate than hard offers. They're easy and risk-free for someone to accept—like asking someone to take an easy step onto the first rung. They can include free audio CDs, Web site content, and tip sheets. A good soft offer is going to appeal to more people because it's relatively painless.

"The reason the response rate is so important," Steve went on, "is that the cost of a print or direct mail campaign is usually fixed. The fewer leads that you generate, the more expensive each lead becomes. For example, let's say you spend $1,000 on a print ad, and using a hard offer you attract 10 leads. Let's assume you close 50 percent of those leads within three months. That means your cost per lead was $100, and your cost per client was $200.

AD ⟶ $1,000

HARD OFFER ⟶ 10 responses

CLOSING RATE ⟶ 50%

CLIENTS ⟶ 5

COST PER LEAD ⟶ $100

COST PER CLIENT ⟶ $200

"Using a different scenario, let's say you spend $1,000, but this time you use a soft offer that attracts 100 leads. Because you used a soft offer, your conversion rate ends up being only 20 percent over nine months. But your cost per lead drops to only $10, and your cost per client to only $50." Steve paused to scribble these numbers on a fresh page of the flip chart.

AD ⟶ $1,000

SOFT OFFER ⟶ 100 responses

CLOSING RATE ⟶ 20%

CLIENTS ⟶ 20

COST PER LEAD ⟶ $10

COST PER CLIENT ⟶ $50

"If each client was worth $3,000," he said, "your sales from the hard offer would only be $15,000. Your sales from the soft offer would be $60,000—four times more than the hard offer! Starting with a soft offer can make a huge difference to your sales, even when you factor in a smaller closing rate."

	HARD OFFER	SOFT OFFER
Responses	10	100
Closing Rate	50%	20%
Clients	5	20
× $3,000	$15,000	$60,000

"I can see how a soft offer will generate more leads," said Ted, rubbing his eyes as he tried to absorb all this new information. "What I don't understand is how a free CD or tip sheet will do anything to personalize my relationship with each lead."

"That's because it won't!" Steve exclaimed. "The point of The Offer is to identify leads before your competition and get them onto the first rung of The Lead Ladder, as well as to help begin to differentiate you as an adviser. The Lead Ladder then combines this first soft offer with harder follow-up offers, such as seminars and consultations, designed to **personalize** your relationship with each lead as they move up the ladder. With each rung, your offers will move from ultrasoft to a little harder, each time becoming more personal, until finally leads reach the top of the ladder and become clients. You will be building relationships with your prospects based on trust and your ability to help them solve The Problem. Will some leads and prospects fall from the first, second, or third rung? Of course. The point is to get as many people as possible to make the climb by taking that all-important first step."

> *The Lead Ladder then combines this first soft offer with harder follow-up offers, such as seminars and consultations, designed to **personalize** your relationship with each lead as they move up the ladder.*

"But how many rungs should The Lead Ladder have?" Ted asked.

"It's different for every business," answered Steve. "Generally, the more expensive or complex the service, the more rungs you'll need. A housecleaning service may need only two rungs—the lead offer and the close—while a consultant specializing in corporate mergers and acquisitions may need five or more rungs. It all depends on how quickly you are able to earn the trust of each prospect. That's why so many salespeople love referrals—it's like a shortcut to the top of the ladder. But relying on referrals for 100 percent of your business is dangerous, as you have recently discovered. Just remember that the goal of each rung is to build that relationship with the prospect, and the appropriate height of The Lead Ladder will become clear.

LESS EXPENSIVE, LESS COMPLEX

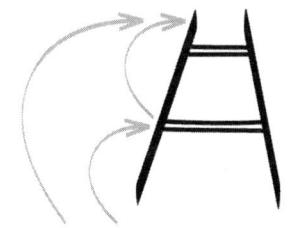

MORE EXPENSIVE, MORE COMPLEX

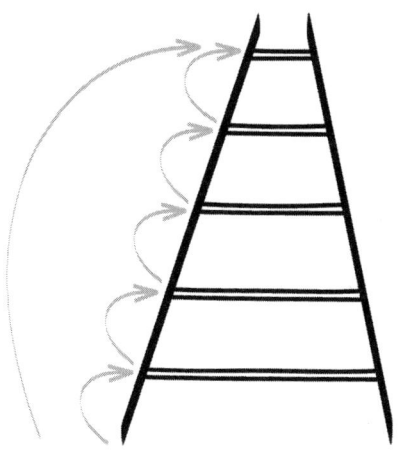

"Also remember that each new step on The Lead Ladder should be relatively easy," Steve added. "The first step, the soft offer, leads to the next step of a phone consultation, for example, which leads to the next step of an office visit, which leads to the next step of a trial membership, which leads to the last step of becoming a client. Each step is an easy trip from the one before. And even with multiple rungs on The Lead Ladder, some leads will leap directly from the first to the last rung and become clients right away. These are people who have a pressing, immediate need for your service and are ready to buy now."

"Yeah," Ted sighed, "you can't get enough of that type of lead—literally!"

Steve laughed. "Soft offers will still attract these highly motivated buyers. But you're right—most people will not move up the ladder so quickly. Slower climbers are not necessarily less valuable. Many will make it to the top, but they will do so on their own time, when they're ready. Try to rush them up too fast, and they'll slip and fall straight back to the ground.

"Also, if you don't give every lead a clear next rung, that lead may get stuck on the first rung. Every step on The Lead Ladder must have a clear call to action and offer—the next rung—in order to keep a lead moving. You can't assume that your leads and prospects will know what to do next. You must always show them the next step."

> *Every step on The Lead Ladder must have a clear call to action and offer—the next rung—in order to keep a lead moving.*

"OK," said Ted as he stared intensely at the flip chart. "I'll use a soft offer first, and then use harder offers for the other rungs of The Lead Ladder. Where do we get started?"

"The first step is to think about what content can help people in your target market solve The Problem," replied Steve. "Start thinking about topics and titles, not detail yet. Try to think of multiple topics and titles at first, and then slowly narrow down your choices to one or two that you feel will be the most compelling for your target market.

"After you've narrowed down you choices for content, you should consider your format options. The choices will largely come down to economics, the numbers of leads you expect to

> *Offer content: Information that will help people solve The Problem*
> *Offer format: How that information is delivered*

receive, and the needs of your market. For example, if you need to generate thousands of leads, then perhaps a free audio or PDF download off your Web site makes sense. On the other hand, if you are dealing with a very expensive service and need to generate only a couple of hundred leads a year, you may consider a fancier print or audio package that you mail to your leads."

Format choices will largely come down to economics, the numbers of leads you expect to receive, and the needs of your market.

Ted was charged up and ready to go. The question of what to offer was now much simpler to answer. He and Steve created rough ideas for follow-up offers that represented ever-higher rungs on The Lead Ladder. Each rung would lead prospects to more personalized offers. They considered follow-up offers such as workshops, seminars, personal evaluations, product demonstrations, and free trials. Finally, Ted decided that his Lead Ladder would have four rungs based on the complexity and cost of his company's service.

Ted took a step back from the flip chart to better see his new Lead Ladder. Each rung was a relatively easy step from the one before it.

The first-rung offer, an information kit, would be a no-brainer for people who suffered from The Problem that the kit offered to help solve. Any potential customer with such a problem would be crazy not to request the kit, in Ted's opinion. There was no downside for them—just the little bit of time and energy to respond to The Offer and then review the kit.

Ted's Lead Ladder

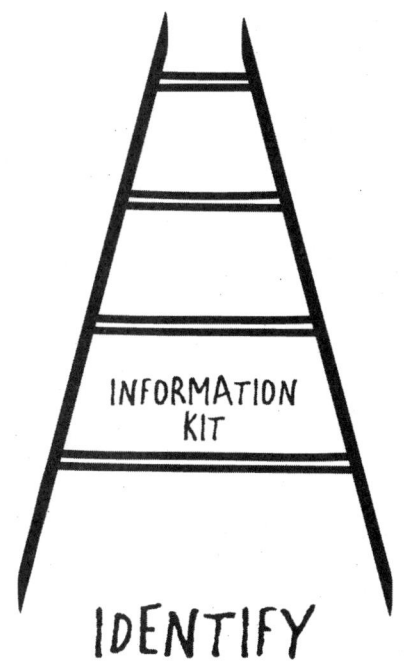

Of course, Ted also knew that many of these leads would never move past the first rung. But he also knew that some would, either immediately or after a few months or even years. If he could **identify** the prospects with The Problem that he solved, and do it before they responded to his competitors' offers, it would be only a matter of time until most of those leads would take the next step up The Lead Ladder.

The second-rung offer, a seminar, would give Ted the opportunity to start solving his prospects' problems in a more personal way. The exchange was simple: Ted would give attendees some more valuable information about solving The Problem, and they would give him the chance to **personalize** the relationship. Anyone who had received and benefited from the first offer, the information kit, would likely take the time to come to Ted's seminar.

The third-rung offer, a personal consultation, went a step further. Now Ted would be using an even harder offer, trading more specific, personalized information than one could get at a seminar, in exchange for a one-on-one meeting. Ted knew that if he could only get his prospects to open up about The Problem, he could then easily demonstrate how his

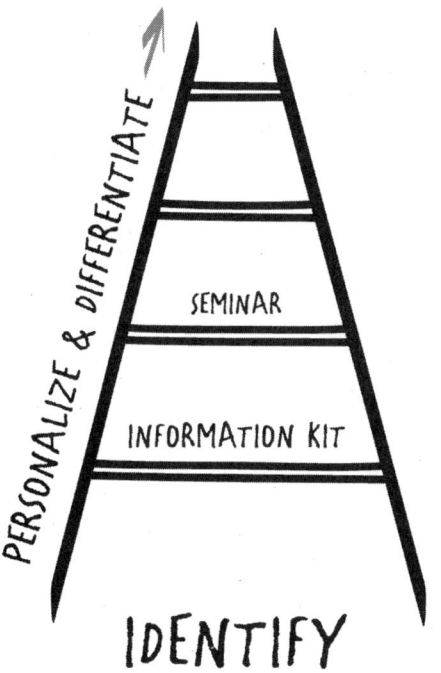

company would solve it and close the deal. Because most of these consultations would be with prospects who had already received the information kit and attended the seminar, Ted would have already **differentiated** himself from other salespeople simply trying to sell their products and services. The atmosphere of the consultation would be relaxed and productive. Prospects who reached this level of The Lead Ladder would be very likely to make it to the final rung and become clients.

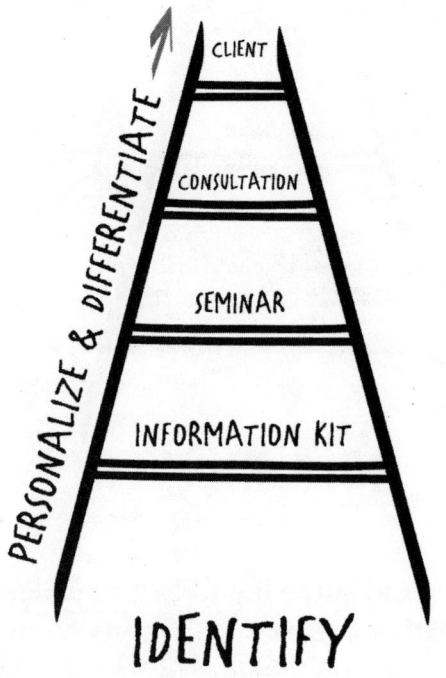

"What I'm still confused about," Ted said, "is that although this approach makes so much sense, how come more companies aren't doing the same thing?"

Steve knew that his friend would raise this point. It was a good question, one that he had often asked himself as he was building his own Lead Ladder for his business. "There are two main reasons you don't see more of this approach with other companies," he began. "The first is simply that this process doesn't appear the same from the outside as from the inside. Most people don't recognize soft and hard offers as being part of a Lead Ladder. We've both been prospects on many Lead Ladders, whether they were called that or something else. In fact, a lot of companies think that they use a similar approach, when really they are still trying to take a shortcut with their prospects, which leads me to the second reason you don't see this approach too often: patience. Everybody is looking for the quick fix, the silver bullet that will bring in a wave of happy paying clients quickly and easily. That's what you tried to do when you placed your full-page ad. You thought that you could simply buy some business with a single-shot approach."

Ted sighed. "You're right. Live and learn, I guess."

"Yes, but I've done that, too," Steve said. "Unfortunately, business doesn't work that way, at least not anymore. Nowadays you must earn your clients' attention and trust, and that doesn't happen overnight. It happens by investing in the long term and sticking with an intelligent, well-thought-out marketing process. The irony is that while this approach is a long-term strategy and does require patience and consistency, using it will still attract ready-to-buy customers, the ones who will leap up the ladder to the top rung. But you will also enjoy the rewards of being patient with equally valuable but slower climbers. And, if you pick the right target market and the right offers, your future sales will be greater than you could have ever imagined."

Nowadays you must earn your clients' attention and trust, and that happens by investing in the long term and sticking with an intelligent, well-thought-out marketing process.

"That's the effect I'm going for!" Ted said, feeling more optimistic than he had in a long time. He knew Steve was right. He had looked for the quick and easy solution, instead of rethinking his approach from the ground up.

By now it was well past dinnertime, and Ted and Steve were both exhausted. They agreed to take the next day off to allow some time to let all their new ideas jell.

CHAPTER 3 REVIEW

Probably the most important aspect of marketing your service is The Offer. Lead generation is all about getting relevant prospects to raise their hands and identify themselves. The best way to get the most people to do this is to create an offer that has value to them and offers The Solution similar to that of your service.

1. Think about the difference between hard offers and soft offers. List all of your current marketing tactics and categorize them as soft or hard offers.

2. How many rungs should your Lead Ladder have? The answer will depend on how expensive and complex your service is:

   - How quickly do you need your leads to be converted into clients?

   - How many separate offers can you afford to create?

3. Review The Problem that you solve. If you plan to use an informational offer such as a booklet, report, or CD, you need to focus on offering The Solution to The Problem.

- What kind of content can you create to help solve The Problem?

- What format would best deliver this content for the first rung? The second rung? The third rung?

Chapter 4

ADVERTISING
Where and How to Market The Offer

When they met up next, Ted already looked worried again.

"What's wrong?" Steve asked, noticing the tension on his friend's face.

"I guess I'm worried about the next step," Ted said. "So far, everything seems to have clicked into place. I've set sales goals, picked a target market to focus on, and come up with some great offers for my Lead Ladder."

"OK, so what's the problem?"

"Well, I'm confused about how I'm supposed to get the word out about The Offer. I mean, where do I advertise this? Do I use direct mail, e-mail, display ads, trade shows? Which is the right choice? And, once I've picked the method, what do I actually advertise—my brand, The Offer, or both? It's just a little overwhelming."

"You're right—it *is* a little confusing," Steve replied. "But before you allow yourself to get overwhelmed, let's break this down into two major steps. First, we decide *what* exactly you're going to advertise. Then we'll figure out *where*. Sound like a plan?"

"Sure," said Ted, shifting in his desk chair. He still felt overwhelmed.

"OK, as far as what to advertise," began Steve, "think about how your ad failed and why. We agreed that it was most likely because the ad was about you, not your customer. Why did you do it that way?"

"I guess because that's what everyone else seems to be doing," Ted said.

"Exactly! One of the biggest problems with your advertising was the role models that you had to choose from when coming up with your own campaign."

"Great—it wasn't all my fault," Ted laughed.

Steve chuckled. "Most advertising that we are exposed to is for large corporations who each spend hundreds of millions to billions of dollars every year to get their messages out to consumers. Because these massive companies need to sell millions of units of product, and they have the budgets to saturate their markets with ads, their ad agencies create slick branding campaigns designed to increase mind share. Compare that to companies selling a specialized product or service to a target market."

"Like us," Ted interrupted.

"Yeah, like us. Can you afford thousands of ads? Of course not. And yet, because of your role models for 'good' advertising, you mistakenly believed that by just combining your logo, name, and a clever slogan, you, too, could build a brand that attracted new clients. Any company looking for immediate and tangible results should be far more concerned with attracting measurable responses to an ad, rather than building mind share or other subjective measures of an ad's success."

Any company looking for immediate and tangible results should be far more concerned with attracting measurable responses to an ad, rather than building mind share or other subjective measures of an ad's success.

"In other words," Steve continued, "you need to focus on creating a direct response campaign that produces leads by advertising The Offer, not your brand. By building your database with solid leads, you'll establish a very powerful brand to a select, but correct, group of people."

"What do you mean?"

"There are basically two types of advertising: *image*, or branding, and *direct response*,"

Steve explained. "The primary difference between direct response and image advertising is that direct response includes a specific offer and a clear call to action that persuades people to act. The goal is a lead, or a sale, or an appointment, or some other specific action. A campaign is either successful or not based on an immediate, measurable response. Rather than just focus on promoting your brand, you should be offering prospects something tangible and specific. By using direct response, you take some control over the process by actually soliciting a response, rather than simply hoping that people will like the look of your ad or tagline and decide to give you a call."

> **Image advertising:** *Advertising that focuses on mass brand familiarity*
> **Direct response advertising:** *Advertising that focuses on generating immediate and measurable results (e.g., leads, sales, inquiries, etc.)*
> **Call to action:** *A specific offer and instruction for receiving that offer (e.g., "Call 1-800-555-5555 to receive your free subscription to _____"*

Rather than just focus on promoting your brand, you should be offering prospects something tangible and specific.

Ted nodded slowly. "So what you're basically saying is that my past advertising followed the wrong model for my budget and needs. I created an image campaign, one that would have needed to be much larger and more diverse in order to even possibly work. With only one ad, my odds of success were tiny. Instead, I should create a direct marketing campaign focused on advertising The Offer and giving people a very clear and specific reason to respond. That way, every single ad or mailer I pay for will be measurable."

"You got it! Whether an ad is underperforming or doing great, you'll know which approach to discontinue and which to pour more energy and resources into.

"Now," Steve continued, "as far as *where* to advertise, let's think back to our original step of setting sales goals. One of the main purposes of that step was to help you figure out an appropriate level of promotion, right?"

"Oh, yeah," said Ted. "Didn't we figure that I would need about 10 clients to reach my goal for the year? And based on a closing rate of 50 percent, I would need to get 20 appointments in order to close those 10 clients. Then we figured that I would need roughly 200 leads to get 20 appointments, and based on a response rate of 1 percent, we estimated that I could generate 200 leads a year by reaching 20,000 people. So I guess the real question is, *how* do I do that?"

"The answer will never come to you until we first have a good idea of your options," answered Steve. "You can't possibly know where to advertise until you know what targeted mailing lists, trade magazines, and Web sites are available to advertise in. You need to take your target market and figure out as many ways as possible to reach them. Then, we need to compare each of these resources to one another in terms of reach, how targeted they are, and cost efficiency. Only then will you be able to narrow down your options."

"OK, sounds like a plan. Where do we start?" asked Ted.

"I know that the library has computer databases, including free access to advertising and marketing resources. Let's start there and see where it leads."

With that, Ted and Steve headed to the library. They enlisted the help of the research librarian, and within a half hour they were accessing hundreds of advertising media and lists. By the end of the afternoon, they had a diverse list of advertising and marketing choices, including mailing lists, opt-in e-mail lists, trade magazines, newsletters, and Web sites that all specialized in exactly Ted's target market.

> **Cost per thousand (CPM):** *If an ad costs $1,000, and it is viewed by 50,000 people, the CPM is $20.*

Steve flipped open his laptop computer and began entering data for all of their choices into a spreadsheet, including the total reach, the cost per thousand, and the total dollar costs of each.

By the time the library closed, Ted and Steve had narrowed the list down to the most appropriate advertising methods for Ted's situation. Ted then called each of these resources for their media kits, which would provide him with even more detail than the library database.

Armed with this new knowledge of several advertising options, Ted felt that what was once a confusing and overwhelming decision was now clear and simple. He now had specific choices, and his job was simply to start with those that made the most sense according to the numbers of appointments, leads, and total reach he would need to make his sales goal.

"What's missing?" Ted asked. He was relieved that they had made so much progress in such a short amount of time, and he was excited to get started with his new marketing approach. But something was still bugging him. He had gotten swept up with The Offer, the target market, and the advertising strategy. "I mean, what do I do with all these leads and prospects once I've got them? How do I get them to move up The Lead Ladder?"

"I know exactly what you're asking," Steve said, "and I agree. If all you did was target your market with a relevant offer, I'm sure that you would attract clients. But you would also be missing out on the majority of future business. Just because The Problem exists, and a prospect responds to The Offer with the hope of solving that problem, doesn't mean that that prospect is going to be ready to move to the next rung on the ladder right away. I mean, any number of things could come into play: personal issues, other business needs, lack of money, or the sudden desire to try to solve The Problem on their own. All of these things could delay a prospect from continuing to climb The Lead Ladder. If all you do is provide The Offer and wait around for something to happen, then only the prospects with the most immediate of needs will contact you and become clients. You'll miss out on all the others who simply got caught up with any number of life's other problems."

If all you did was target your market with a relevant offer, you would be missing out on the majority of future business.

Ted nodded. "So what do I do about it?"

"The way I see it, there are only two things missing," replied Steve. "Once you build those last two parts into your system, you will have what it takes not only to attract clients now but also to reap the benefits of your marketing efforts months and even years into the future."

CHAPTER 4 REVIEW

Advertising, direct mail, networking—these are some of the tools you can use to get your offer out there and generate leads. Before you can decide which approach makes the most sense for your business, you must be aware of all your options.

1. Go back to your answers in chapter 1. How many leads do you need to generate each year? Is the number high or low?

2. Based on your answer to question 1, which kind of marketing approaches make most sense? Remember that the more leads you need, the larger your reach needs to be.

3. Are you currently using image advertising or direct response?

4. What's your current return on investment for every dollar that you spend on advertising or direct mail?

5. Visit your main branch library, and ask to use the Standard Rates and Data Services (SRDS) database, if available. This service is what advertising agencies use to find advertising media for their clients. Several other databases are available as well, including ones detailing print advertising, online media, and mailing lists. You can search by industry classification or keyword, and print out the results for each search. You should be able to find a wealth of marketing options that you are probably not currently aware of. Each printout gives most if not all of the information you need to know about an advertising medium, including circulation and costs of each ad size.

6. Review your options from your research of the SRDS. What approach would make the most sense to start with based on the cost and targeted nature of the advertising medium or mailing list?

CHAPTER 5

THE DATABASE
The Future of Your Business

It was now well after dinnertime, but Steve knew that Ted was on the verge of a real breakthrough. Rather than go home and lose their momentum, they ordered a pizza and ate in Ted's office. When they finished eating, Steve stood up, stretched, and started drawing on the flip chart.

"Are you ready for the next round?"

"You bet," Ted said, wiping his mouth with a napkin.

"Assuming that some leads will move up The Lead Ladder faster than others," Steve began, "we need to make sure that you capture every lead as it comes in so that not a single one is wasted. Basically, you need to build a database. While today's clients are important, focusing on long-term prospects is key. It's all about timing, about

> *Database: An organized and actionable list of leads, prospects, and clients*

getting people up The Lead Ladder at their own pace, until they finally become clients. To systematically nudge people up The Lead Ladder, you must have an organized list that shows where each lead is so that you can get them to the next step. In other words, you need to invest in a practical contact management software program with specific features to help you build relationships with more prospects and convert them into high-paying clients."

> *To systematically nudge people up The Lead Ladder, you must have an organized list that shows where each lead is so that you can get them to the next step.*

Ted nodded. "You read my mind. My biggest concern was that I would get caught up with just the faster clients and forget all about my other leads."

"Yes," Steve agreed, "and of course, this is what most salespeople do. They focus only on the most promising leads and prospects because they haven't built a systematic approach to tracking leads. Sure, they may keep some business cards handy or maybe a list of 'interested' people. But that's where it usually ends.

"Obviously, the most basic part of your database will be contact information: name, address, phone number, and e-mail address. But in addition to that, in order to build a database that's a real asset to you, now and in the future, you'll also need to record and manage specific pieces of information so that you'll have the best chance of moving more people up The Lead Ladder.

"Like what?"

"Beyond the obvious contact information, you'll need some way to identify where each person is on The Lead Ladder," Steve explained. "More than likely you'll have at least three basic categories: leads, prospects, and clients." He jotted these words on the flip chart.

"*Leads* are people who have requested The Offer or more information about your service. They can also be new contacts you meet while networking or speaking, or a referral from a friend or client. A *prospect* is someone who you have established some level of personal connection with. A *client* is anyone who has paid for your service or product.

"You'll also want to track the source of each contact. How did they hear about you? From an ad, a mailer, word of mouth? Create groups of contacts based on their source so that you can gain a clearer picture of which aspects of your marketing are working and which aren't. That way, you can commit more time and money to the winners and multiply the effectiveness of your marketing as a whole.

> *Create groups of contacts based on their source so that you can gain a clearer picture of which aspects of your marketing are working and which aren't.*

"Finally, whatever software you use, it must make it easy to assign a set of follow-up activities to every new contact. For example, you can assign different activity series based on where each contact is on The Lead Ladder. Follow-up for prospects on the third rung will be different than follow-up for fresh leads. By creating different activity series first, then linking them to each new contact, your follow-up tasks will be automatic and much easier to execute."

"That makes sense," Ted commented. "But for how long do I do these follow-up tasks?"

"There should be no limit to the length of time you can automatically schedule follow-up activities," replied Steve. "That way, you'll have no reason not to continue following up periodically for a year or even more. After all, you have already succeeded with the expensive task of getting each lead onto the first rung of The Lead Ladder. Follow-up, on the other hand, is extremely inexpensive. Not organizing each and every lead for long-term follow-up is like throwing away money. Most leads who become clients will sometimes take weeks or months to climb to the top of The Lead Ladder. Your database is your investment into your future success, and as it grows will be one of the most valuable aspects of your business."

Not organizing each and every lead for long-term follow-up is like throwing away money.

"I sure can see how that would be the case," Ted said. "Anything else I should have in this all-important database?"

"You bet. Since the goal of The Lead Ladder is to create more personal relationships with potential customers, you'll need to include important information about each person in your database. Everything you know about each lead should be saved, including specific problems they face and competitors that they've used. You can even include things like their birthdays, a favorite author or movie they've mentioned, or a hobby. Just make sure that everything is instantly accessible. If all goes well, you will be talking to a lot of people every day, and you'll find it very difficult to remember the important details about each one of them without a little help."

"I definitely see how valuable all this information could be," Ted said, "but isn't it cheating to keep track of personal details on a computer? I mean, aren't I trying to trick people into thinking that I effortlessly remembered all this information about them? Won't it be obvious?"

"First of all," Steve replied, "just because you happened to write down the name of someone's dog, for example, doesn't mean that you now try to figure out some clever way of working it into the conversation. It's not about tricking anyone. It simply comes down to preparation. The more you know about someone and his or her own unique situation, the more easily you can help that person solve The Problem. And, remember, too, that most of the information you keep may never come up, but it's better to be prepared in case it does."

> *The more you know about someone and his or her own unique situation, the more easily you can help that person solve The Problem.*

"So then I don't have to say things like, 'How's the golf game, Stan?'" Ted asked with a grin.

"Of course not," Steve chuckled. "Transparent rapport-building clichés like that are the exact opposite of how to build a real relationship with people based on trust. Just be yourself, but be prepared. Nothing more than that."

Ted sighed with relief. It was finally all coming together. He felt like every bit of doubt and anxiety about the future was lifting from his shoulders. Suddenly, it was clear that nothing could prevent him from being successful again.

"OK," Steve said, "remember how I said there were two parts missing? We just covered one of them—organizing your leads in a database. The last piece is simple. In fact, it's probably the easiest part of the whole process. You just need to do it consistently, even when you're busy or feel like you don't have the time. Do this last thing well, and you'll be able to hit almost any sales goal you set for yourself."

CHAPTER 5 REVIEW

Most of your lead generation efforts will be wasted without a simple, easy-to-use, and automated way to store and retrieve information on prospects and other contacts. Many software programs are available to help you keep everything organized and ensure that you are able to consistently follow up and convert more leads into clients.

1. How are you currently organizing your leads?

2. If you don't already own one, purchase a software package for contact resource management (CRM).

3. Consider organizing your leads and prospects as follows:

    - Every time you get a fresh lead, immediately enter it into your database. Be sure to include all of the contact info you were given, as well as the source of the lead (referral, ad, mailer, etc.), and any other grouping or classification that will help you keep your prospect list organized.

- Immediately assign a follow-up schedule to the new contact. Most software programs have a feature that makes it easy and fast to schedule multiple follow-ups (calls, letters, etc.). How and when you follow up will be covered in the next chapter.

4. Make it a daily habit to check your calendar for any scheduled follow-up activities. Remember that consistency is the key to converting leads into clients. Software makes it easy to automate the scheduling of your follow-up marketing, but you must still follow through every day in order to see results.

Chapter 6

FOLLOW-UP
Turning Strangers into Clients

Ted took his friend's bait. "What's the last part?"

"It seems like common sense," said Steve. "The last part of this really does come down to simple execution. Think about all the companies that collectively spend millions of dollars to get their messages out to potential customers. Letters and mailers are sent; ads are published and broadcast. A small fraction of those efforts pay off in the form of leads. Prospects call for more information and the company sends it. What happens then?"

"Usually nothing, I'd say," replied Ted.

"Right. After all that effort and time and money, the irony is that too many companies simply leave their leads twisting in the wind. They are literally forgotten about. As a result, fewer leads turn into clients. Only those people who are very interested in buying soon even speak with a salesperson.

"Lead generation is not all it takes to turn strangers into clients," Steve continued. "It is just the first, albeit essential, step. It simply identifies those people with The Problem that you solve. Generally, the softer The Offer, the more leads you will attract. But few will turn into clients without consistent follow-up to move them up The Lead Ladder until they reach the top and become clients."

Few people will turn into clients without consistent follow-up to move them up The Lead Ladder until they reach the top and become clients.

"So we know that the right database program will make it easy to plan, schedule, and execute my follow-up," Ted said. "What I need to decide now is exactly *how* to follow up."

With that, Ted and Steve spent the rest of the night planning Ted's exact follow-up steps. Ted knew that at any time he could adjust his plan—all its parts were flexible. But he also knew that he needed to start somewhere, and by two in the morning, he and Steve had drafted an easy-to-execute set of follow-up activities. With the right database, Ted could inexpensively and easily follow up with every single lead he generated. Never again would he be able to use the excuse that he didn't have the time to follow up, and as a result Ted knew that his future business from current leads would be large and very profitable.

Every single follow-up would be designed to get each lead to the next rung of The Lead Ladder. In Ted's case, everybody on his first rung—those people who had requested an information kit—would receive follow-up letters inviting them to Ted's seminar, the second rung. People on the second rung—those who actually attended the seminar—would receive

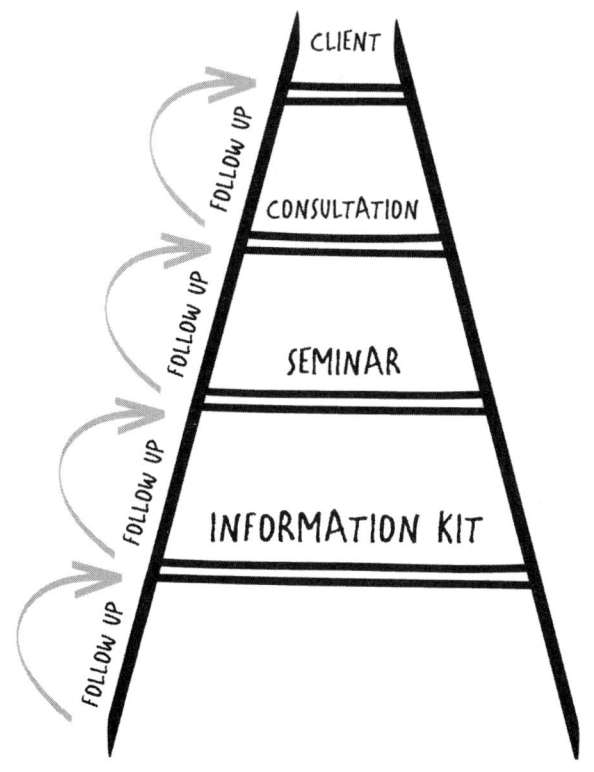

follow-up phone calls to see whether they'd like a one-on-one consultation, the third rung. Ted felt very optimistic that during the more personal consults, he could nudge prospects pretty effortlessly to the last rung, where they would become paying clients.

Every single follow-up would be designed to get each lead to the next rung of The Lead Ladder.

Ted knew that it didn't really matter how long it took each lead to make it up The Lead Ladder. Every person would be different and would make the climb at his or her own pace. Ted could do very little to speed the trip. What he could do, however, was make sure to follow up consistently. Without constant and focused follow-up, leads would get stuck on the first rung, most of them forever. He was confident now, however, that such an outcome wouldn't be the case for his business.

CHAPTER 6 REVIEW

To ensure that more people move up your Lead Ladder, you must follow up consistently with offers that motivate people to act.

1. Think back to all the leads and inquiries you've gotten during your career. Have you followed up consistently with each and every one of them? If not, why? What were some of the obstacles preventing you from keeping up with all of your leads?

2. Which follow-up methods appeal to you? For example, if you are comfortable calling prospects, maybe telephone follow-up would work. If you are more comfortable with mailers, follow-up letters and postcards might make the most sense. There is no right or wrong answer. What matters most is that you pick an approach that you will use *consistently*.

3. How many times are you willing to follow up with a lead? Remember that many leads and prospects won't become clients for a few months, but none of them will become clients if you give up too soon and stop following up with them. A good rule of thumb is following up at least 10 times over 2 years. The cost is negligible, and an organized follow-up system combined with a prospect database should make it easy to keep up.

4. Remember, the goal of each follow-up is to get the lead to move to the next rung of The Lead Ladder. Very rarely will a lead go from requesting The Offer to hiring you on the spot. Often, there are many steps in between that must be taken. More specific information, phone consultations, and face-to-face meetings may all be needed to further *differentiate* you as an adviser while *personalizing* your relationship with each prospect. Your follow-up should simply nudge each person along to the next rung.

Chapter 7

THE SUCCESS STORY

Over the next few weeks, Ted began to execute his new plan. At the beginning he found himself having to adjust his approach as he experimented with new ideas and new markets, but the system kept him focused.

He remembered that in order to painlessly turn strangers into clients, he would need to

- **identify** leads before his competitors did;
- **differentiate** himself as an adviser, not a salesperson; and
- **personalize** the process by giving people a good reason to let him into their lives.

Ted knew that he would need to adjust his own definition of successful marketing. Rather than simply measure success in one huge step or just by an immediate income jump, he learned to draw satisfaction from each smaller step. He celebrated every new lead, every time a lead moved up The Lead Ladder, and of course, every time a lead made it to the top and became a client. This last step happened infrequently at first. Ted received some immediate business from his new campaign, but relatively little compared to the total number of leads he received.

Nevertheless, he maintained his focus. He continued to target his niche market, refine The Offer and follow-up offers, and experiment with new and different advertising strategies, constantly trimming off the losers and reinvesting into more effective methods. He built his database, one person at a time, being careful not only to enter new contact information accurately but also to maintain and update contacts as they moved up The Lead Ladder. And he continued to follow up consistently. Every call was made; every letter was sent. As a result, more and more leads turned from strangers into prospects and then clients as they reached the top of The Lead Ladder. Ted faced fewer rejections, instead enjoying a much more pleasant rapport with prospects than he could ever have hoped for.

Now, only six months later, Ted's Lead Ladder had hundreds of people on it. Most were still at the first rung, but many were higher up, and plenty of prospects were positioned directly below the top client rung. He had already passed his original client goal and was on track to more than double it by the end of the year. Once again, business, and life, was good.

Chapter 8

APPLYING THE LEAD LADDER TO YOUR SPECIFIC SITUATION

Ted's dilemma at the beginning of the story is not an uncommon one. More than likely, you've experienced the same kind of frustration that comes from trying to market and sell a service using the wrong approach. As you can see, the solution is neither simple nor easy; it takes a lot of effort, planning, and patience to painlessly turn strangers into clients. The good news is that anyone can do it, as long as you're willing to take the time to earn the trust of your leads, prospects, and clients.

This book was written to help walk you through the process of building your own Lead Ladder. Since every business and situation is unique, it is important to interpret for yourself how each step relates to you and your particular needs. There is no one-size-fits-all approach to building a Lead Ladder for your business. It starts with understanding what it is you want, who you need to reach, and what it is that *they* want. Once you know those answers, you can begin to plan your strategy.

To illustrate the flexibility of The Lead Ladder, let's look at three specific situations: real estate sales, sales management, and new businesses.

THE LEAD LADDER FOR REAL ESTATE PROFESSIONALS

Today's real estate professional faces enormous challenges—market forces that will only get more chaotic in the future. For residential specialists in particular, the monopoly on information that they once enjoyed is now gone forever. Home buyers and sellers are no longer dependent on real estate professionals for access to market information and listings. Now anyone with a computer can access virtually every home for sale in any market around the country.

Adding to this challenge are the numbers of new entry-level agents. The long real estate boom of the past few years has introduced a whole new generation of competitors. Supply and demand is now thoroughly out of whack. The supply of real estate expertise is at an all-time high, while demand from buyers and sellers for market information from these professionals is at an all-time low. To compete, real estate professionals need to make themselves far more valuable to home sellers and buyers by offering information not easily found elsewhere.

It's no wonder that many real estate agents list referrals as their primary means of attracting new business. We know from Ted's story that referrals are important but limited; one cannot control all the steps necessary to attract them consistently. Most brokers and agents who do actively market themselves do so through largely ineffective image advertising. Take, for example, a typical real estate professional's postcard campaign, which usually consists of a name, a photo, a tagline, and a phone number. Very few listing agreements originate this way.

Real estate professionals who fail to consistently identify, differentiate, and personalize will find themselves facing shrinking incomes, longer workdays, and job-related burnout. The Lead Ladder offers an alternative method for those who struggle to attract clients using outdated, ineffective marketing strategies. Again, there is no quick fix, no shortcut to building relationships with lots of prospects. The sooner you start to look at your business from a different perspective, the sooner you can get on with the work necessary to succeed in spite of the challenges facing the industry.

> *The Lead Ladder offers an alternative method for those who struggle to attract clients using outdated, inefficient marketing strategies.*

Common Marketing Strategies of Real Estate Professionals

Chances are that you already engage in some kind of active marketing to generate leads. Also likely is that each marketing approach is at best moderately effective. Let's go through the most common approaches, compare them with the elements of the Lead Ladder, and see where you may need to adjust your approach.

Newsletters and Postcards

There are now available many types of newsletter and postcard templates, designed to be customized and mailed out to home owners. Again, most of these are used as image pieces, featuring a photo and name of the agent, a tagline, and a phone number to call "any time." A specific offer rarely exists.

Identify: Newsletters that are mailed to a raw list of homeowners do not help you identify those most in need of your service. By simply mailing it to everyone, you have done nothing to narrow down your market to the most likely candidates. You also have done nothing to get them to call you first, before your competitors, by offering them something that people at the early stages of their decision-making process would really want.

Differentiate: There was a time when a newsletter was considered novel and different. No longer. Template services and computer programs make it easy for most agents to mail out their own newsletters. The more agents who use the same approach, the less it sets you apart. Same goes for postcards.

Personalize: Because typical newsletters and postcards have no clear offer or call to action, they give home owners no reason to invite you into their lives. The only offer generally used is a free personal market analysis, which often requires too much commitment from the home owner at such an early stage. Why would someone invite a total stranger into their home, particularly when they know that person will try to sell them something they're not yet sure they want?

Because these newsletters and postcards do nothing to identify the best leads before your competition, differentiate you as a trusted adviser, or personalize the relationship through follow-up offers, they ultimately fail. Remember that nearly everyone else is offering a "free market analysis." This approach doesn't set you apart.

Cold Calling

Cold calls used to be effective. But with new limitations on phone soliciting, placing unsolicited calls to home owners on "do not call" lists is illegal and punishable by fine. This fact alone should exclude cold calling as a plausible marketing approach. There are, however, plenty of other reasons to avoid cold calling.

Identify: Cold calls are also generally made to raw lists. Again, time is being wasted on people who have in no way identified themselves as having a specific need.

Differentiate: What part of a cold call doesn't scream "salesperson"? It certainly doesn't differentiate you as a trusted adviser.

Personalize: Not only do you have the pressure of creating rapport over the phone through an unsolicited call, but you also usually have to do so at dinnertime. Good luck. Most cold callers do little more than annoy the recipient—the last thing you want to do when trying to earn a person's trust.

Planning Your Lead Ladder

Goal Setting

Most of your listings will fall within a broad value range, and your commission will change depending on the split; therefore, your average value per client may be difficult to project. Rather than focus only on total revenue goals to determine your client goal for the year, consider instead using a transaction goal (e.g., 15 closings per year).

Target Market

Keep in mind that the larger your sales goal, the larger your market needs to be. Because you are limited to a local area, if you do decide to specialize in a specific niche market, it needs to be large enough to support your target goal.

Offer

Because the goal of The Offer is to *identify* home sellers and buyers before they meet with another agent, your offer should relate to the early process of selling or buying a home—namely, gathering information and evaluating choices. By offering this information free of any commitment, you will attract more leads than your competitors that you can then *personalize through a follow-up offer.*

Advertising

Resist the temptation to make your mailings about yourself. This approach will entail a difficult transition for some agents, since "image building" has been a common practice for so many years. The key problem in this case is that it does nothing to *differentiate* you from everyone else using the same strategy. By focusing your promotions on clients' needs, you will be attracting more relevant leads with whom you can build a highly personalized and effective brand.

Database
An up-to-date, accurate database is the most important asset you have. In real estate, the turnaround time from lead to listing can be months or even years. The more people you are able to manage on your Lead Ladder, the more listings you will get. It's that simple. Trying to manage this process without a database tool like CRM software is a recipe for disaster.

Follow-up
Following up with leads is by far the easiest and cheapest part of the process. The cost of attracting a lead is much higher, yet most agents spend all of their time prospecting for new leads at the expense of their relationships with current leads. Be different. Don't just go after the same low-hanging fruit that everyone else is chasing. Take the time to follow up with more personalized offers, and cultivate your own orchard.

THE LEAD LADDER FOR SALES MANAGERS

Regardless of your company's industry, size, or specialization, your sales team's ability to painlessly turn strangers into clients and identify, differentiate, and personalize will have a direct impact on their success and longevity. Sales managers who expect their teams to rely on cold calling are risking not only low revenues but high turnover as well. The more control you want over sales targets, the more important it is for you to give your people the tools that they need to succeed.

The greatest challenge that a sales manager needs to overcome to implement a Lead Ladder successfully in a sales department is collaboration with the marketing department. In order to generate quality leads for your sales team consistently, your marketing department must coordinate an effective direct response campaign as well as manage leads until they are handed off to your team.

> *The greatest challenge that a sales manager needs to overcome to implement a Lead Ladder successfully in a sales department is collaboration with the marketing department.*

The purpose of advertising should be simple: to generate sales leads. How each company specifically strives to achieve that goal is a likely source of debate between its marketing and sales departments. Your own marketing department may be focused only on creating brand awareness, leaving lead generation up to the sales team. More than likely, your marketing people feel that a strong brand will make it easier for your team to prospect for new clients. Unfortunately, because most brand-based advertising is ineffective, it wastes a tremendous amount of marketing capital while adding little value to the selling process.

The problem is magnified when marketing and sales act as separate departments, each with its own agenda. This stance has to do more with internal politics than with sound business sense. Regardless of the reason, it's critical to implement a change and align the goals of both departments in order to get a higher return on your company's marketing investment. Of course, if you are in charge of both sales and marketing, then you are in the perfect position to ensure the most effective approach.

Aside from creating the right materials and offers for your Lead Ladder, you must clarify which department is responsible for each part of the marketing/sales process. Again, if sales and marketing operate as one, this role assignment will be easy. The challenge arises when there is disagreement between the two departments as to when marketing ends and sales begins.

Generally, marketing departments like to focus only on producing and distributing advertising, direct mail, and other promotions. Their job ends when the ads go out, and any leads and inquiries are directed straight to the sales department. Sale teams, on the other hand, prefer to be handed leads only after they have been qualified. The less qualified the lead, the more time, effort, and rejection is involved for the sales team. Of course, the closer to the top of The Lead Ladder a lead is, the more interested a salesperson will be in that lead.

The appropriate handoff point of each lead is up to you and your associates. It can be different depending on variables such as department size and type of product or service offered. In any case, there should be a clear mandate as to who is responsible for every step on the ladder. For example, a four-step ladder could look something like this:

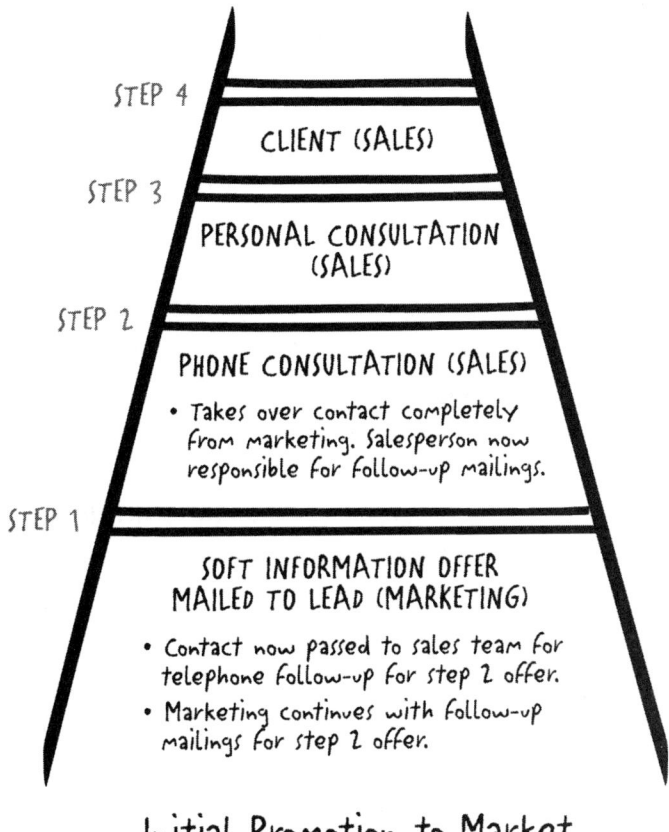

As you can see, this Lead Ladder includes a specific point where leads are handed over from marketing to sales, as well a step at which both departments maintain some ownership over each lead. The sales team takes over the more personalized steps, while the marketing department continues following up until each lead is firmly in the hands of the sales department.

> *This Lead Ladder includes a specific point where leads are handed over from marketing to sales, as well a step at which both departments maintain some ownership over each lead.*

The benefit of this approach is simple: no lead goes unpursued. If you waste a single lead between marketing and sales, you risk wasting all of them. Nothing will destroy the ROI of a marketing campaign more quickly. The Lead Ladder will work if all of the steps are consistently maintained, and that will happen only if your sales and marketing teams work closely together in the pursuit of this common goal.

THE LEAD LADDER FOR A NEW BUSINESS

If yours is a brand-new business, either your own or one that you work for, you are in the unique position to create a lead generation campaign from the ground up. Free of the conventions and habits from the past, you can work on developing the best strategy for your budget, market, and product.

Resist the temptation to start spending money on any advertising or direct marketing until you have first established your sales goal, target market, offer, advertising strategy, database, and follow-up strategy. Without these elements in place, you will simply be spending money blindly. If you are keeping your overhead reasonable, there is no reason to waste precious capital on a weak strategy.

The challenge for most new businesses is that picking a target market and offer can be very difficult. Established companies have the benefit of hindsight to help them determine which choices make the most sense. If you are finding it too difficult to pick one target market, feel free to improvise and experiment with two or even more at once. The same goes for offers, advertising methods, and follow-up strategies. Regardless of the age of your company, creating a marketing plan is only the first step (see the appendix). Just because you pick a certain target market for starters doesn't mean that it is the best choice for the long term. It simply means that based on the information you have, that particular target market makes the most sense at the time.

You will be far better off picking targets and strategies based on educated guesses than simply relying on random luck. Every marketing dollar that you spend needs to provide a healthy return on your investment if you expect to succeed. That said, the rewards of your early efforts may not be financial but educational. Trying a specific, measurable approach, even if it isn't successful, can give you tremendous insight and experience that you can then directly apply to future strategies. It's all a learning process, but starting with a plan will make it much easier, and cheaper, to figure out what will and won't work for you.

APPENDIX
Creating Your Marketing Plan Step-by-Step

Your marketing plan does not need to be a thick document full of graphs and data to be effective. What you do need is a guideline for what to do, when to do it, what questions to answer, and other details that will make it much easier to find clients.

The previous chapters have provided an overview of what you needed to do to build The Lead Ladder. Now you're going to look at your own unique situation and create a plan that incorporates all of these pieces into one clear strategy.

Remember, a marketing plan is not a static tool that you create once and forget about. It needs to be maintained, reviewed, and adapted as your situation changes. This blueprint is just a starting point, and as time goes on and your business or market changes, you will need to continue to make adjustments to get the best results possible.

STEP 1: DEVELOP YOUR CLIENT GOALS

1. What is your client goal for the next 12 months?

2. Based on your answers in chapter 1, how many leads will you need to generate to reach your client goals?

STEP 2: TARGETING YOUR MARKET

1. Based on your answers from chapter 2, list some of your niche opportunities based on

   - industry,
   - size,
   - past experience, and
   - potential.

2. Narrow down these choices to no more than three or four.

3. Did you do your homework and check out the SRDS database at the public library? Based on your research, which of your market choices has the most advertising or direct marketing opportunities?

STEP 3: CREATE YOUR OFFER

1. Based on the target market you chose, what type of offer would people in that market be most interested in?

2. What format will your offer take (e.g., tip sheet, CD, download, consultation, etc.)?

STEP 4: SELECT YOUR ADVERTISING

1. Based on your research on the SRDS, how will you reach your target market with your offer? Will it be through online or print advertising, or through direct mail or some other form of direct response marketing?

STEP 5: BUILD YOUR DATABASE

1. Purchase a good software program to track your leads.

2. Enter data for every lead, prospect, and client you get from now on:

    - All their contact information—name, business name, address, phone and fax numbers, and e-mail address

- Their source—referral, cold call, response to ad, and so forth

- Their position on The Lead Ladder—lead, prospect, or client

3. Once you devise your follow-up methods in the next step, be sure to come back to your database to create activity series.

STEP 6: DESIGN YOUR FOLLOW-UP SYSTEM

1. Which follow-up methods will you use?

2. What will your follow-up offers be to nudge your leads up The Lead Ladder?

3. How often and for how long will you follow up with each lead?

ABOUT THE AUTHOR

Marcus Schaller is the founder of Purple Dot Group, a lead generation strategy consulting and publishing firm. He has more than seven years of service marketing experience in real estate, consulting, and consumer and business services.

Marcus lives in New York City with his wife, Emily, and son, Sam. You may reach him directly at marcus@purpledotgroup.com.

For your free subscription to *The Lead Ladder™ Letter*, or for information about Purple Dot Group's workshops and seminars, visit **www.leadladder.com**.